The Courageous Lion in MiLo

By Myles B. Nobles, M.S., CCC-SLP

This book is dedicated to the following people:

To my mother, Ronetta Suber, my father, Derrick Nobles, and brother, Collin Nobles. And to the love of my life, Tony Shavers III, who inspired and encouraged my creative thoughts, ideas, and the vision of turning my book, into a reality.

This Book Belongs To:

....

....

Age : ....

Today was Monday, but not a regular Monday.
It was presentation week!
Milo didn't want to go to school.
He woke up from a bad dream.
Milo dreamt that his whole class laughed at him
during his presentation.

"Good morning, Son," Mommy said."You're running late. It's time to get ready for school."
"But Mommy, I don't want to go to schoow this week."
"Why not, Son?" Mommy asked."You must."

"Well, Mommy... it's presentation week!
I have to present fun facts to the cwass about
my favorite animaw—the wion."
"Milo... the word is class, not cwass, the word
is animal, not animaw, and the word is lion,
not wion. Remember your 'L' sound."

"I know, Mommy, but it is so hard to say."
"I know you'll do great," Mommy said.
"Remember to take a couple deep breaths
before you begin speaking to calm your body."
"Okay, Mommy, I wiw."
Milo had missed the bus, so his mommy drove
him to school.

When Milo's mommy pulled up to the school,
she gave him a big hug and kiss on his head.

"Have a great day, Son! Good luck on your presentation."

As the school day began, Milo's teacher, Ms. Jones, wrote two words on the board, in all capital letters:

"Hello class," Ms. Jones said. "For presentation week you will share five fun facts about your favorite animal. You will be called upon randomly, so get ready! Our first student is... MILO."

Milo walked to the front of the class.
He covered his mouth with his paper
of fun facts.

Milo remembered
that his mommy told him
to breathe before speaking.

He took three deep breaths and began...
"My favorite animaw is a wion
because it is the king of the jungwe."
He looked up and saw his classmates
starting to laugh at him.

When Milo got home from school that day,
his mommy could tell he had been crying and
asked what was wrong.
"My cwassmates waughed at me because
I can't say the 'W' sound,
You know what I mean.
I don't want to go back."

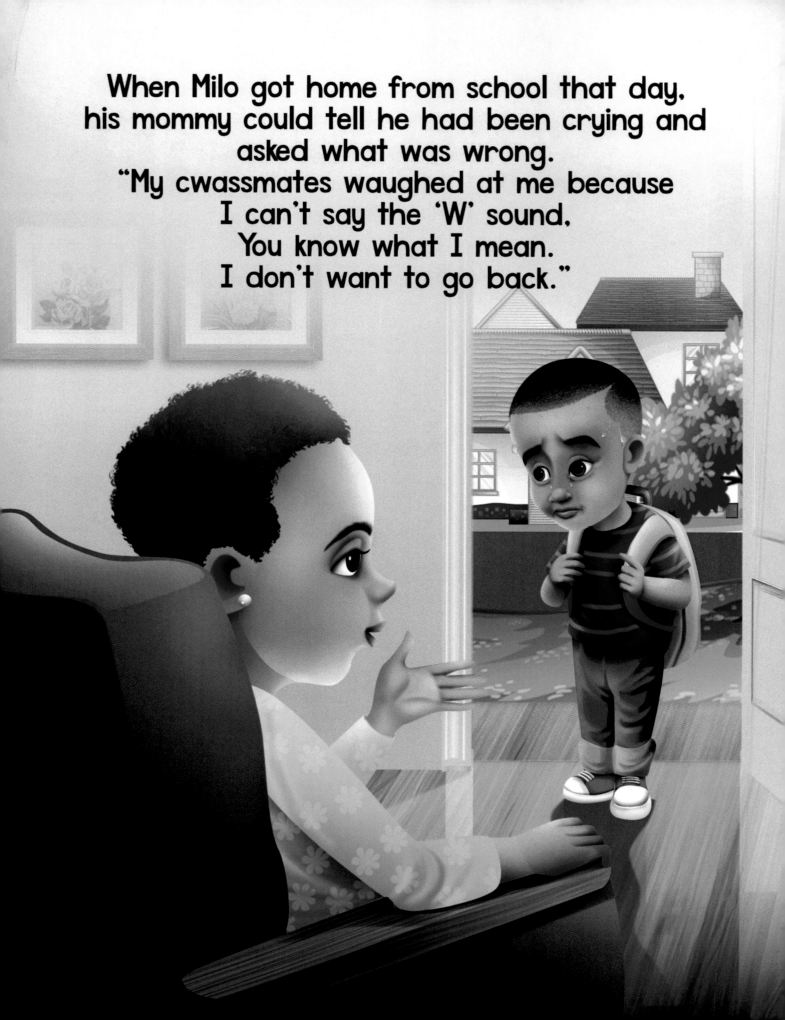

That night, Milo's mommy told him...
"Son, people will talk and laugh behind
your back until you're old and gray.
This is the first time, but won't be the last.
Don't let others steal your joy.
Instead, prove them wrong."

Milo asked his mommy for help.
She said,"Of course baby.
Mommy will always have your back."
"Get some rest and we will deal
with this in the morning."

The next day, Milo's mommy scheduled a meeting with Milo's school's principal, his teacher Ms. Jones, and the Speech-Language Pathologist, Mr. Nobles.

After the meeting was over,
Milo's mommy told him that he was going to see
the speech teacher,
Mr. Nobles, a couple of times a week for
the next two months. They were going to
practice the"L"sound together.
He also told Milo that after he completed
Speech Therapy, he would have to finish
his presentation to receive his final grade.

Mr. Nobles became one of Milo's favorite teachers.
He was so nice during Speech class.
Milo got to play board games, and received
stickers and treats if he participated and did well.

Mr. Nobles said the most important part of pronouncing "L" is to place your tongue just right. Using Mr. Mouth, he showed Milo how to curl the tip of your tongue and touch the bumpy spot on the roof of your mouth behind your two front teeth.

He then showed Milo again by doing it himself and saying "L." After, he asked Milo to try.

Milo was super nervous. But Mr. Nobles had a surprise to help. He gave Milo one of his favorite snacks: Peanut Butter!!

Mr. Nobles placed some peanut butter on the roof of Milo's mouth, right on the bumpy spot. Mr. Nobles told Milo to curl the tip of his tongue and touch the peanut butter.

After a few tries, Milo was able to do it! Once he understood how he was supposed to place his tongue, Mr. Nobles said it was time to try making sound.
He gave Milo a countdown from 3...2...1, and it was like magic! He was able to say "L" with peanut butter in his mouth. Milo was so happy and amazed!! He couldn't believe it.

After a week of using peanut butter to help Milo say "L" by himself...
It was time for a new approach.
Without peanut butter, Mr. Nobles asked Milo to say "L." He did it! He was surprised and proud of himself.

Now Milo practiced saying the letter "L" in words, phrases, sentences, and then in conversation.

After a couple months, Milo achieved all his speech goals and graduated from Speech class!

The next day, it was time for Milo to redeem himself.
Ms. Jones called Milo to the front of the class...He took a few breaths and began to present his favorite animal.

"Good morning, my name is Milo, and today I will be presenting on my favorite animal, the Lion." "The Lion is my favorite animal because it's the King of the Jungle!" Milo noticed that his classmates were paying close attention and not laughing at him. By the end of the presentation, he received a round of applause from Ms. Jones and the class.

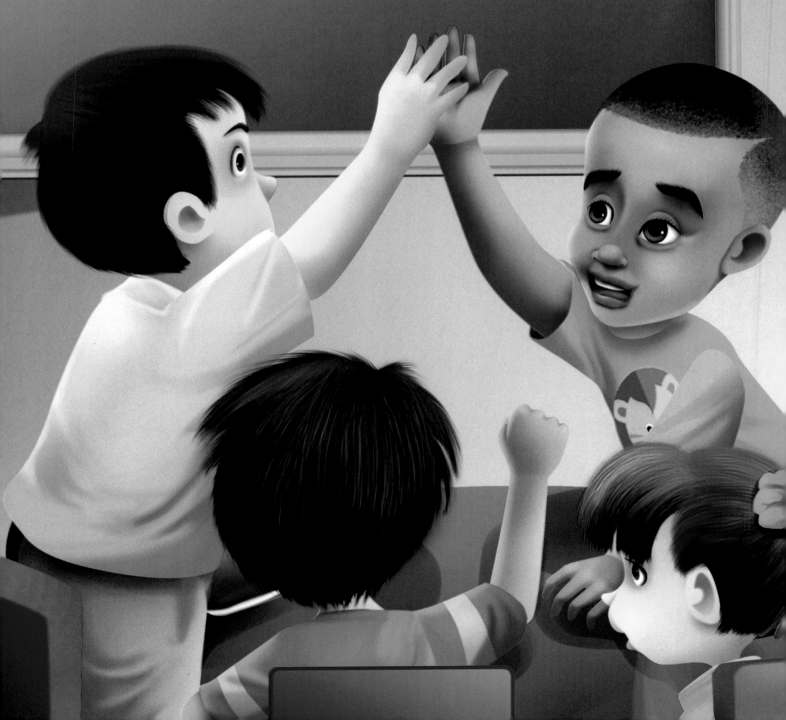

Ms. Jones said, "Job well done, Milo! A+"
Milo couldn't believe that all of his
hard work had paid off!! He realized
that he could do anything through patience,
persistence, and perseverance.

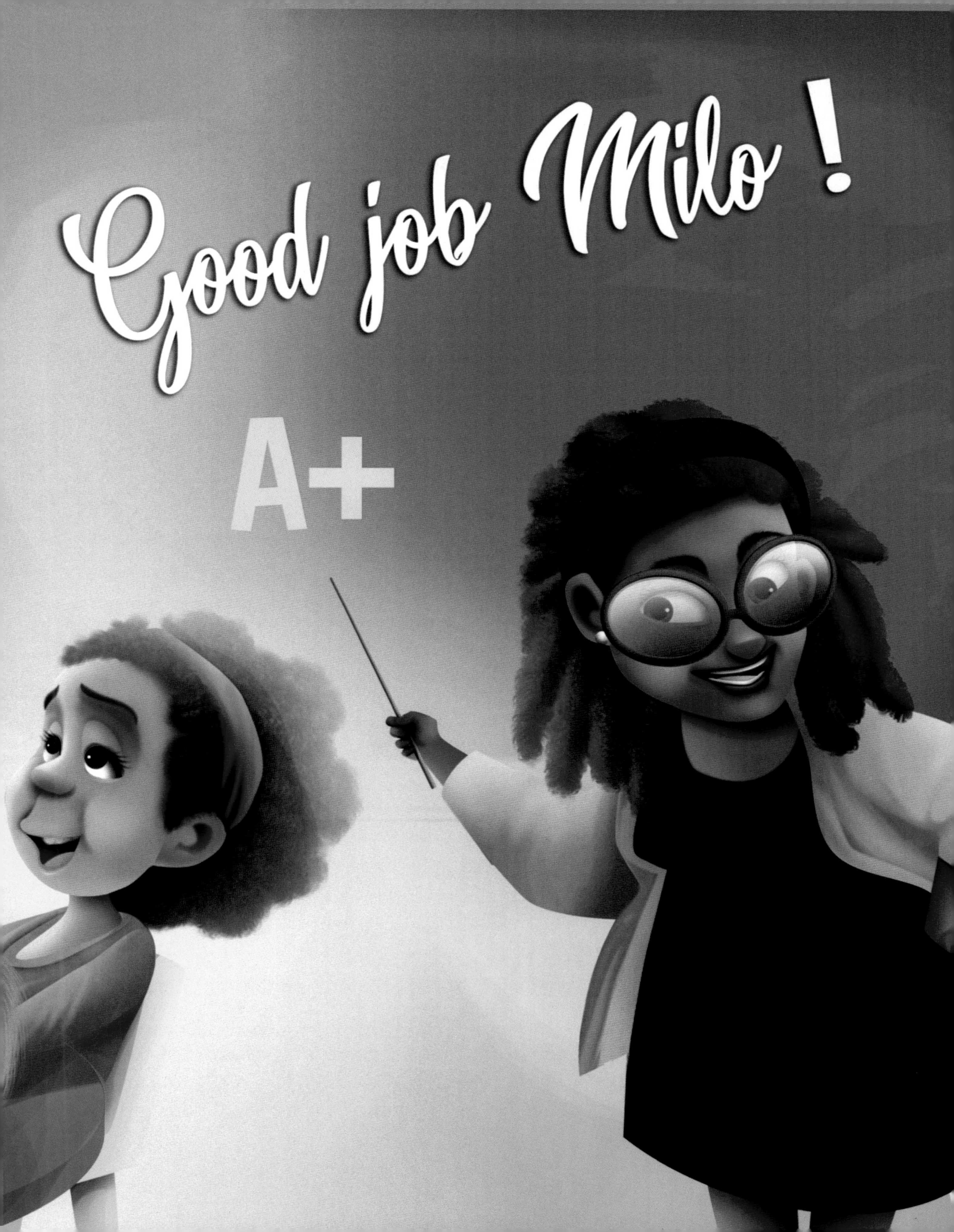
Good job Milo !
A+

Words to Learn from Milo

1.Amazed [uh-meyzd] (Verb) - To surprise greatly or fill with wonder

Sentence: Milo was so happy and amazed!! He couldn't believe it.

2. Courageous [kuh-rey-juhs] (Adjective) - Brave

Sentence: The Courageous Lion in Milo

3. Favorite [fey-ver-it] (Adjective) - Liked over all others

Sentence: The Lion is my favorite animal because it's the King of the Jungle.

4. Goal [gohl] (Noun) - A result or end that a person wants and works for

5. Graduate [graj-oo-eyt] (Verb) - To receive a pass on completing a class in school

Sentence: After a couple months. Milo achieved all his speech goals and graduated from Speech class!

6. Nervous [nur-vuhs] (Adjective) - Being fearful or anxious in a specific situation.

Sentence: Milo was super nervous. But Mr. Nobles had a surprise to help. He gave Milo one of his favorite snacks: Peanut Butter!!

7. Participate [pahr-tis-uh-peyt] (Verb) - To take part in or share

Sentence: Mr. Nobles became one of Milo's favorite teachers. He was so nice during Speech class. Milo got to play board games.and received stickers and treats if he participated and did well.

8. Patience [pey-shuhns] (Noun) - The ability to stay calm

9. Persistence [per-sis-tuhns] (Noun) - The act to continue to do something even though it's hard or other people are against it

10. Perseverance [pur-suh-veer-uhns] (Verb) - To continue in a course of action, task, or belief.

Sentence: Milo couldn't believe that all of his hard work had paid off!! He realized that he could do anything through patience, persistence, and perseverance.

11. Pronounce [pruh-nouns] (Verb) - To make the sound of or express with the voice in a specific way.

Sentence: Mr. Nobles said the most important part of pronouncing "L" is to place your tongue just right.

12. Random [ran-duhm] (Adjective) - Made or done without purpose or pattern; made or done by chance.

Sentence: "Hello class," Ms. Jones said. "For presentation week you will share five fun facts about your favorite animal. You will be called upon randomly, so get ready! Our first student is... MILO."

13. Redeem [ri-deem] (Verb) - To make up for; balance.

Sentence: The next day, it was time for Milo to redeem himself.

14. Speech-Language Pathologist (Noun) [speech] - [lang-gwij] [pă-thŏl'ə-jĭst] - A trained individual that helps people improve their communication

Sentence: The next day, Milo's mommy scheduled a meeting with Milo's school's principal, his teacher Ms. Jones, and the Speech-Language Pathologist, Mr. Nobles.

Made in the USA
Columbia, SC
08 February 2022

55761991R00024